CAROL MOBLEY

HOV
PUBLISHING

What Pain Changed
"Living Life Again"

Unless otherwise noted, Scriptures are taken from the New King James Version®. Copyright © 1982 by Thomas Nelson. Used by permission. All rights reserved.

HOV Publishing a division of HOV, LLC.
www.hovpub.com
hopeofvision@gmail.com

Front Cover Design by Hope of Vision Designs
Inside layout by Hope of Vision Designs
Editor/Proofread: Phyllis Bridges for Harvestseed Collections

Contact the Author, Carol Mobley at mobleycarrol@gmail.com

For further information regarding special discounts on bulk purchases, please visit www.hovpub.com

ISBN Paperback: 978-1-955107-32-7
ISBN eBook: 978-1-955107-31-0

Printed in the United States of America

Dedication

First and foremost, to my children, I love you and appreciate every time you checked on my well-being. I never would have survived all the years of pain without you two with me.

Second, I thank my close family and friends for allowing me to vent and cry on their shoulders. I love you all and appreciate our talks. Last but not least, I thank my publisher and mentor for the push to purpose. I love you all dearly!

WHAT PAIN CHANGED

"LIVING LIFE AGAIN"

CAROL MOBLEY

Contents

Preface

God has been listening to your prayers. He has felt your uncertainties, frustrations, confusion, and pain. He sees the tears you shed at night for your family, friends, and those you love and care about. For every tear you have cried, there is a blessing.

You are coming out of this; the pain will end. You are being shaped and made during all you have gone through and are experiencing. God will open doors no man can close, even in this season of uncertainties. Beloved, be ready for your shift. Greater is coming! Embrace the powerful transformation of who you are becoming in Christ Jesus. Receive it and trust God's timing in your life.

Chapter 1

What Pain Changed

"What Pain Made" evolved to become a means for me to share the story of pain in my life, which I never expected. I had to learn that pain will make you or break you. Pain will cause you to be bitter or better; either way, it is not easy. Pain will cause you to lose focus on the most important thing in your life: YOU.

I was made through every painful situation, and now it is time to live healed, truly blessed, and in peace. Despite every obstacle I may face in this lifetime, I will always know that Jesus loves me and provides for me. He also speaks to my spirit and leads me daily. I will trust in the Lord during difficult and challenging times of change. Change may be uncomfortable, but it is needed to reach my divine destiny. God said, Carol, it is time for change. I am changing and becoming the real and better version of me. I am changing in the storm. I am rising above everything the enemy sent to destroy me, and I am winning. I am an eagle; I spread my wings and fly high above it all. To soar, I had to remind myself who I am and whose I am.

I thank God for the peace of change. Everything I endured was for my good, and once I realized it, I desired better for my life, and I held myself accountable.

To grow and progress, you must be willing to give up some things. You cannot continue to allow people and things to control how you see yourself.

I refused to succumb to pain and hurt. I overcame pain and hurt. I became an overcomer to every obstacle that tried to take me down. Growth is a process, and as I grew, I saw so many things in life that I had to stop doing to move forward. I have a purpose, and no one can change that. It does not matter what they think they see in me; I know who I am in Christ. I am enough to do his will. I am okay with being Carol Mobley. I refuse to be anyone else to please people. God is the only one who truly knows me, and He accepts me. I know I am highly favored by the Lord. I am chosen, and I know God loves me. So be careful how you treat me; be extremely careful what you say about the people of God.

I have grown from what pain made to what pain changed, and I will never be the same again.

Chapter 2

Change is Necessary

Change is a word that so many fear; I certainly did. I was so comfortable with life as it was that I became comfortable even in the pain. You may wonder why I became so comfortable. Well, when you are used to a thing, even though it needs to change to get better, you begin to go along with it. Even though you have dealt with it year after year, you stay in it because you are comfortable. It does not matter how much it hurts, you will stay there because not only have you gotten comfortable, but you are afraid to move on, or you do not want to start over. It seems easier to stay. Just a few years ago, that was me. Because I had been married for so long, I settled and compromised. I forgave him so much I was blue in the face. It was clear that the more I forgave, the more it seemed he took me for granted and that it would not change. I had to make a choice.

I can proudly say that I did all I could do to make my marriage work. January 2022, I challenged myself to change and improve everything, including my relationship with my husband and others. I made the choice to choose ME. I am at peace with my choice. I am free to do everything Christ called me to do. I will no longer let anything stand in my way. I raised my children to be great human beings, and today, I live with love for Christ first and self-love, with everything else following. It was a long time coming, but change has come.

Change never comes easily, but through faith and personal growth, I have learned to let go and let God control my life. This is not just my story, but my prayer for you. Yes, I had to endure some pain to become who I am today. Those experiences shaped me into someone who can share and help others. I'm so thankful that all things come to an end. Now, I'm in a season of promise and prosperity. I refuse to let the enemy keep me in a shell or make me feel inferior. I am powerful beyond measure! I speak this with the authority and power of Jesus Christ, my Redeemer. I know my Redeemer lives! This is my season of change, and I believe everyone connected to me will also experience victory. I hold onto this belief with all my heart, and no one can say or do anything to make me feel different. I yearned for love for so long, not realizing it was always there for me from Christ, my children, family, and true friends. Their love and support were my anchors in the storm. I am not saying my husband did not love me, but his actions made me question his love for me. I still love him and always will, but that part of my story is over unless something changes.

I am a firm believer that love is what love does. If you love someone, you will do right by them no matter what. I know Jesus loves me; there is no doubt about it. He showed love for all when he gave His life for us on the cross. I love hard and true; even when it hurts, I love unconditionally. No one can ever take that from me. As I always say, "I know what I bring to the table, and I am not afraid to eat alone." Trust me when I say that the peace of God is such a blessing. I never imagined such peace existed for me, but it does! And I am so grateful and glad about it! I always fixed myself up on the outside because I love myself. It's a different kind of love when you truly fix yourself up on the inside by letting go of things you cannot control and loving yourself more. It's a love that renews, that empowers, that heals, that transforms and restores.

My journey of change was not easy, but it was worth it. I am worth the love I feel for life as I embrace this new journey of singleness and strength. Ladies and Gents, embrace your singleness and strength, and know you can no longer settle for whatever comes. We have the power to shift the norm, and speak greater into our lives, because we know that we are loved by the best, Jesus Christ. We will no longer fear change. With the authority and power Christ has given us, let's proclaim, "I Made the Choice to Choose ME!"

The verb change means: 1. To make (someone or something) different; alter or modify. 2. Replace something with something else newer or better;

substitute one thing for another. The noun change means, the act or instance of making or becoming different; to undergo transformation.

As we age and encounter life, we should eventually want to see change. Change is necessary.

WHAT PAIN CHANGED

"LIVING LIFE AGAIN"

CAROL MOBLEY

Chapter 3

Let Go of Emotions

Emotions can cause a painful inner conflict and delay when they fight against God's guidance. I recognized God's voice, and I obeyed when He told me, "Let him go." But my emotions, my deep-rooted feelings of so many years together led me astray into disobedience. I found myself in a conversation with God and myself, "Lord, he knows me, I know him;

Lord, I am too old for all of this," I pleaded. I was accustomed to his touch and presence; I could not bear the thought of being with anyone else. So, I stayed connected to him in any way possible.

Please understand, that God will give you the desires of your heart even when it is not necessarily what you need. Believe me when I say there were good days, bad days, and happy moments, but the pain was slowly increasing, and still I was willing to go through it. I wrote volumes 1 and 2 of What Pain Made during this time. Life seemed pretty good for a while. However, when I wrote volume 3, I experienced a significant shift in my circumstances. It was like a whole 360-degree turnaround filled with pain. I remembered what the Lord said years ago, "Let him go!" That's all I can remember the Spirit of the Lord saying. I am not embarrassed by him returning to his old habits. However, I am ashamed that I was walking in disobedience, yet wanting and expecting everything to work out. Please understand, we cannot walk in disobedience and expect blessings.

WHAT PAIN CHANGED

"LIVING LIFE AGAIN"

CAROL MOBLEY

Chapter 4

Solitude

Solitude is a state of being alone without being lonely. It's about finding peace and contentment within yourself without needing external stimulation. Solitude is not about avoiding being with others, it's about being with yourself and becoming intimate with your mind and true essence. Loneliness, on the other hand, is a sense of emptiness, a feeling that something is missing, and a need for company, even if it's not what's best.

When you truly understand and embrace your worth, you set a standard for how you demand to be treated. You refuse to accept anything less than you deserve. When the best arrives, please do not compare it to those who have hurt you and undermined your self-worth. The best will love you as you have always deserved to be loved.

Yes, pain has been a part of my journey, but it has also motivated my personal growth and resilience. I have become unbreakable by reaffirming my relationship and trust in God, practicing self-love, and choosing to prioritize myself. I've learned to value, protect, and revel in the peace, freedom, and insight into my true self, which I've discovered in my moments of solitude. These moments of self-reflection have become my guide, helping me to set and pursue personal goals, both short and long-term. My quiet space has become a sanctuary for progress enabling me to make necessary and God-led changes.

My solitude is refreshing and replenishing my soul and sharpening my thoughts. I can think more clearly than I have in a long time. I can shut out the world's noise and the negative voices that try to undermine me. But remember, solitude is not a circumstance. It's a choice that you must make for yourself. One that can empower you to regain a positive perspective and control over your life, and most importantly, renew you to face life's challenges with a sense of hope and peace, and guide you back to living on your own terms.

I am alone but not lonely; there is a difference. Solitude restores while loneliness depletes. Believe me when I say my alone time has helped me understand myself better. I love myself, and I love the God within me. I used to ask God why I had a heart to help so many who would not do the same for me. In my alone time with the Lord, I realized that I possess the gift of love. When I was looked over by so many, they never saw the value in me, and that is fine. What others see in me is less important than what my Savior sees. He knows me inside and out and thought I was worth saving. So why is everyone else so judgmental when it comes to God?

While I may not speak in tongues like others, I communicate in English with positive, pleasant, and encouraging words whenever I have the opportunity. A person's character tends to go a lot farther than anything else. I have learned a lot about myself in my alone time, and I am so much more than what others see. Some may underestimate me, but I will never give up. I am a warrior for Christ, and my determination is unwavering. I will never try to be like anyone else. Also, I firmly believe in trying the spirit by the spirit. I can discern others' feelings when they are around me, so do not think it strange of me if I wean myself from some individuals. My solitude has allowed me to have healing, restoration, growth, forgiveness, and profound newness. I can see clearly now that the pain is gone.

I encourage every individual to find a place of solitude where you can recognize the voice of God and truly see yourself. This is where your transformation begins. Take the time for self-evaluation and in time witness the power you hold to change for the better.

Chapter 5

It is Worth It

My transformation was far from easy, but it was so worth every struggle. I never imagined I could survive being so alone while in a relationship with someone. I want to help the next person conquer their fear of being alone and stop allowing unpleasant things to take place to be with someone who is not meant to be in their life.

I endured months of tears during my transformative time. I always wanted my family of four, and for too long, I was willing to accept horrible pain to keep it, so it was painful to know after all the years, tears, and prayers, it was over. However, this pain was bitter-sweet. During the divorce, I had sadness within but a smile on the outside. The process was hard and painful. Now, it was worth it all.

Although I am a strong woman, I needed someone to encourage me through this change. I thank God for my children, Kendra and Marcus, for continuously checking on me and making the transition much easier. Their phone calls and texts to make sure I was alright were all I needed. I thank and appreciate them for being there for me. Also, I thank God for my sister-in-love, Annita, for taking the time to encourage me. I called and texted her so much. I don't know what I would have done without her encouraging words, prayers, and the songs she sent me. My sister-in-love, I love you more than you will ever know. It means so much to have someone you can confide in and never hear what you shared with them from anyone else.

I hope my story helps someone make the right decision for their life. Transformation can be challenging but it is so worth it. It requires some alone time to get to know yourself. Each day becomes easier to deal with once you break free from the struggle. It is like when someone dies, you miss them, but you accept the fact that they are gone, and you keep on living. I am truly living again and loving every minute. I have broken away from what was and welcome what can be. Waking up every morning knowing God has given me another chance to live is so wonderful. As I close my chapter of pain, I open a chapter of change; with great expectation, I breathe again. For the rest of my days, I will embrace my dreams of peace and live how I was meant to. Pain made me; it also changed me, and I will never be the same.

Chapter 6

Time Heals all Wounds

I cannot thank God enough for keeping my mind through this life-changing new beginning. I am free to love myself without regret or induced guilt. After dealing with relationship drama for so long, I became so used to it that I began to accept it as a way of life. Thank goodness for God's healing power, deliverance, restoration, self-love, and discovery! Now, I am so content with myself that although I could date, I can't imagine thinking about it and choose not to. For 30 years I loved intensely and gave my all to my husband, children, and others. Somehow, I should have included myself in that equation.

Now, I give my all to God and myself! It's incredible to know I will not hurt myself anymore. That's right, I said, "I will not hurt myself anymore." How amazing it is to be able to trust myself with me! See, I allowed the pain to happen repeatedly in my life. I lowered my standards trying to keep a marriage that died years before. I hope this helps someone; you must value yourself as God does. God created us in His image. So why don't we see ourselves as He does and realize we are valuable? Often, it is because we allow people we trust into our personal space, and they belittle us or make us feel insignificant compared to them. When all the while, we thought we were in love and being loved. So, we humble ourselves and give our all, but too often with little to nothing in return. For me, this was true. Even in other relationships, there were times when I felt belittled, but never spoke up, which caused others to disregard or sideline me. Now, I don't care what anyone says or does trying to belittle me. Why? Now, I know who I am and to whom I belong. God created us all differently; we were not intended to be the same. Anyone that doesn't like it will have to take it up with God. My clothes, hair color, and style do not determine my relationship or love for Christ. I understand modesty and will never let people put me in a box because our styles differ. Is your character Godly? Can people see Christ in you? That should matter. People will come as they are, and Christ is the only one who can change them. We must love and talk to people respectfully. It is that simple.

I am an original creation of God. So, I will not pray, worship, serve, or dress like others, but what I render will be pure and respectful unto the Lord. I will not lower my values to date or mess around with anyone. As I said earlier, I learned to love myself and embrace change in solitude. The time I spent alone was simply the best thing I've ever done for myself. Self-care is essential for both men and women to have healthy and productive dating. After ending a relationship, it's crucial to take the time to heal before getting into a new one. Time heals all wounds. Sometimes, our outward appearance looks healed, but our insides need healing. The unhealed portion of us will emerge when someone says the wrong thing or pushes the right button the wrong way. For us to walk in true victory, true healing is required. Remember, it does not deserve our time, energy, or effort if it does not generate peace, purpose, or profit. Let today be day one of your new beginning. You can live again! Do not dwell on the past; look forward with excitement for your new beginning.

WHAT PAIN CHANGED

"LIVING LIFE AGAIN"

CAROL MOBLEY

Chapter 7

Single and Satisfied

Becoming truly single and satisfied with my new status took me a while. Although I initially thought I would not, I survived the days alone. If we are honest, no one expects their marriage to fail. However, if it does, our initial response is clouded by not wanting to be alone, even though we would be better off alone.

As I had to, you must change your thinking, open

your mind to new experiences, and know your life will continue. If I never have another man, I am good with that. I am still whole because it is the Lord that completes me. I have such peace and satisfaction with the new me. I will continue to build my enterprise with my family and giving God the glory due to Him. God is my sustainer, comforter, and provider. I owe Him my all. I am healed and free from all the pain; I am embracing my life and living for myself again. I am alone and truly alone. I do not have a man on the side, an undercover or any secret lover, and I am happy. I am totally in love with myself. If I could describe the peace that I have in a way that you could truly grasp, you would desire solitude to discover your own. It is amazing! I no longer settle; I command what happens by loving my God and myself wholly and unapologetically. I only accept what God sends, which are blessings upon blessings. My newfound freedom from settling and receiving God's blessings has liberated me and filled me with gratitude for the life I am living.

My friend, remember that you have the power to choose who enters your life and how they contribute. Do not let anyone withdraw without making deposits, as it will lead to a negative balance; and this is true in any relationship. So, when something unfavorable things happens, instead of shutting down and closing your book, turn the page and write a new chapter on your terms.

WHAT PAIN CHANGED

"LIVING LIFE AGAIN"

CAROL MOBLEY

Conclusion

Broken but Healed

I can honestly say through all the pain I have endured, none compares to the ache I've experienced because of the recent death of my ex-husband, Greg. His death came by surprise and hit with a resounding blow that hurt so deeply while I was still healing from the pain of our marriage. I don't wish this on my worst enemy. I couldn't sleep, I was so overwhelmed with sadness and confusion; I never expected it. I'm glad that I loved him sincerely with a pure heart, without any other intentions. I have no regrets because I did my part during our marriage and even after the marriage ended. It's the constant thought of him that keeps me awake. Despite his faults, I loved him and never stopped loving him, even after the divorce. I'm grateful that I shared that with him before he passed away. He took with him a part of me that I can never regain. I truly hoped he would change, and we would reconcile one day. I never anticipated that he would leave me forever. He was my friend and my children's father; although divorced, we talked every day. Death truly changes so many things. When my mother died in 2014, I lost a part of me, and in 2023, when Greg passed, another piece of me was taken. Too often, this is how life goes.

People offered so much advice but never on how real love feels: aches, pains, and hurts. Sometimes, I wanted to scream, "No, I am not ok! Yes, I still cry about it!" The process of grieving and healing takes time and work. If you have not experienced this, should your time come, you will find out that it is not easy to overcome. But through my relationship with God and Christ, I'm finding healing in my brokenness, strength in my weakness, and joy in my sorrow. I'm a living testimony to the power of God's love. Thank you, Jesus, for making a difference in my life!

I can only imagine how Christ may have felt when He gave His life for the world to have a more abundant life. We were filthy and did not deserve His love; nevertheless, He loved us. Unfortunately, many still trample on Christ's love as if it does not exist. I remember the love I gave Greg and the pain that came with it. We say we want to be like Jesus, but do we truly understand what that means? Christ was persecuted for our faults, but He did nothing wrong. He hung on the cross, shed his blood, and died for a confused and hurtful world. He suffered unimaginable pain. The question is, "Can I, can you stand the pain?" Will we endure as good soldiers of Christ, or will we talk about it but not genuinely be about it? We must be careful not to speak vain words because we will be held accountable and tried in the fire. To be like Christ, we must show others love and do this not just when things are good, but especially during challenging times, and without any agenda. The Bible says, "God is love." Minus the love, grace, and mercy of God, we are a hopeless case and an empty place. My plea is for you to love fiercely, intentionally, and genuinely. Learn to forgive quickly and hold no grudges to ensure that you are free from guilt should your loved one, friend, or whomever passes away before you see or speak with them. Cherish the fond memories and good times you shared with loved ones and friends who are gone. These memories are a treasure that testify to the love you shared. You only get one life but many lessons, please learn from them. Choose to Love unconditionally and remember this question: What would Jesus do? Be blessed!

WHAT PAIN CHANGED

"LIVING LIFE AGAIN"

CAROL MOBLEY

About The Author

Carol Yvonne Barron Mobley, born in 1970 and raised in Baxley, Georgia is a woman of unwavering faith. She is the 7th child of seven children born to the late Clarence & Geneva Barron. In 1992, she married Gregory Leon Mobley, a union that lasted 30 years, and blessed them with two beautiful children, now adults. Despite a recent divorce, Carol's faith in the Lord remains unshaken. She is the Author of What Pain Made, volumes 1, 2, and 3, available on Amazon. Pain has been a significant part of her journey, but it has also been the catalyst for her remarkable personal growth and resilience. She is not bitter; she chooses to be better!

JOURNAL

WHAT PAIN CHANGED JOURNAL:

_____

_____
_____
_____
_____
_____
_____
_____
_____
_____
_____
_____
_____
_____
_____
_____
_____
_____
_____
_____
_____
_____
_____
_____

WHAT PAIN CHANGED JOURNAL:

_____

_____

_____

_____

_____

_____

_____

_____

_____

_____

_____

_____

_____

_____

_____

_____

_____

_____

_____

_____

_____

_____

WHAT PAIN CHANGED JOURNAL:

WHAT PAIN CHANGED JOURNAL:

_____

_____
_____
_____
_____
_____
_____
_____
_____
_____
_____
_____
_____
_____
_____
_____
_____
_____
_____
_____
_____
_____
_____

WHAT PAIN CHANGED JOURNAL:

_____

_____
_____
_____
_____
_____
_____
_____
_____
_____
_____
_____
_____
_____
_____
_____
_____
_____
_____
_____
_____
_____
_____

WHAT PAIN CHANGED JOURNAL:

_____

_____

_____

_____

_____

_____

_____

_____

_____

_____

_____

_____

_____

_____

_____

_____

_____

_____

_____

_____

_____

_____

_____

WHAT PAIN CHANGED JOURNAL:

_____

_____
_____
_____
_____
_____
_____
_____
_____
_____
_____
_____
_____
_____
_____
_____
_____
_____
_____
_____
_____
_____
_____

WHAT PAIN CHANGED JOURNAL:

_____

_____
_____
_____
_____
_____
_____
_____
_____
_____
_____
_____
_____
_____
_____
_____
_____
_____
_____
_____
_____
_____
_____

WHAT PAIN CHANGED JOURNAL:

_____

_____

_____

_____

_____

_____

_____

_____

_____

_____

_____

_____

_____

_____

_____

_____

_____

_____

_____

_____

_____

WHAT PAIN CHANGED JOURNAL:

_____

_____
_____
_____
_____
_____
_____
_____
_____
_____
_____
_____
_____
_____
_____
_____
_____
_____
_____
_____
_____

WHAT PAIN CHANGED JOURNAL:

_____

_____
_____
_____
_____
_____
_____
_____
_____
_____
_____
_____
_____
_____
_____
_____
_____
_____
_____
_____
_____
_____

WHAT PAIN CHANGED JOURNAL:

_____

_____

_____

_____

_____

_____

_____

_____

_____

_____

_____

_____

_____

_____

_____

_____

_____

_____

_____

_____

_____

WHAT PAIN CHANGED JOURNAL:

_____

_____

_____

_____

_____

_____

_____

_____

_____

_____

_____

_____

_____

_____

_____

_____

_____

_____

_____

_____

_____

_____

WHAT PAIN CHANGED JOURNAL:

_____

_____

_____

_____

_____

_____

_____

_____

_____

_____

_____

_____

_____

_____

_____

_____

_____

_____

_____

_____

_____

_____

_____

_____

WHAT PAIN CHANGED JOURNAL:

_____

_____

_____

_____

_____

_____

_____

_____

_____

_____

_____

_____

_____

_____

_____

_____

_____

_____

_____

_____

_____

_____

_____

_____

_____

_____

WHAT PAIN CHANGED JOURNAL:

_____

_____

_____

_____

_____

_____

_____

_____

_____

_____

_____

_____

_____

_____

_____

_____

_____

_____

_____

_____

_____

_____

WHAT PAIN CHANGED JOURNAL:

_____

_____
_____
_____
_____
_____
_____
_____
_____
_____
_____
_____
_____
_____
_____
_____
_____
_____
_____
_____
_____
_____

WHAT PAIN CHANGED JOURNAL:

_____

_____

_____

_____

_____

_____

_____

_____

_____

_____

_____

_____

_____

_____

_____

_____

_____

_____

_____

_____

_____

_____

_____

_____

_____

WHAT PAIN CHANGED JOURNAL:

_____

_____

_____

_____

_____

_____

_____

_____

_____

_____

_____

_____

_____

_____

_____

_____

_____

_____

_____

_____

_____

_____

WHAT PAIN CHANGED JOURNAL:

_____

_____
_____
_____
_____
_____
_____
_____
_____
_____
_____
_____
_____
_____
_____
_____
_____
_____
_____
_____
_____

WHAT PAIN CHANGED JOURNAL:

_____

_____

_____

_____

_____

_____

_____

_____

_____

_____

_____

_____

_____

_____

_____

_____

_____

_____

_____

_____

_____

_____

WHAT PAIN CHANGED JOURNAL:

_____

_____
_____
_____
_____
_____
_____
_____
_____
_____
_____
_____
_____
_____
_____
_____
_____
_____
_____
_____
_____
_____

WHAT PAIN CHANGED JOURNAL:

WHAT PAIN CHANGED JOURNAL:

_____

_____

_____

_____

_____

_____

_____

_____

_____

_____

_____

_____

_____

_____

_____

_____

_____

_____

_____

_____

_____

_____

_____

WHAT PAIN CHANGED JOURNAL:

_____

_____

_____

_____

_____

_____

_____

_____

_____

_____

_____

_____

_____

_____

_____

_____

_____

_____

_____

_____

_____

WHAT PAIN CHANGED JOURNAL:

_____

_____

_____

_____

_____

_____

_____

_____

_____

_____

_____

_____

_____

_____

_____

_____

_____

_____

_____

_____

_____

WHAT PAIN CHANGED JOURNAL:

_____

_____
_____
_____
_____
_____
_____
_____
_____
_____
_____
_____
_____
_____
_____
_____
_____
_____
_____
_____
_____
_____

WHAT PAIN CHANGED JOURNAL:

_____

_____

_____

_____

_____

_____

_____

_____

_____

_____

_____

_____

_____

_____

_____

_____

_____

_____

_____

_____

_____

_____

_____

WHAT PAIN CHANGED JOURNAL:

_____

_____

_____

_____

_____

_____

_____

_____

_____

_____

_____

_____

_____

_____

_____

_____

_____

_____

_____

_____

_____

_____

WHAT PAIN CHANGED JOURNAL:

_____

_____

_____

_____

_____

_____

_____

_____

_____

_____

_____

_____

_____

_____

_____

_____

_____

_____

_____

_____

_____

WHAT PAIN CHANGED JOURNAL:

_____

_____

_____

_____

_____

_____

_____

_____

_____

_____

_____

_____

_____

_____

_____

_____

_____

_____

_____

_____

WHAT PAIN CHANGED JOURNAL:

_____

_____

_____

_____

_____

_____

_____

_____

_____

_____

_____

_____

_____

_____

_____

_____

_____

_____

_____

_____

_____

_____

_____

WHAT PAIN CHANGED JOURNAL:

_____

_____

_____

_____

_____

_____

_____

_____

_____

_____

_____

_____

_____

_____

_____

_____

_____

_____

_____

_____

_____

_____

_____

_____

WHAT PAIN CHANGED JOURNAL:

_____

_____
_____
_____
_____
_____
_____
_____
_____
_____
_____
_____
_____
_____
_____
_____
_____
_____
_____
_____
_____
_____
_____
_____

WHAT PAIN CHANGED JOURNAL:

_____

_____

_____

_____

_____

_____

_____

_____

_____

_____

_____

_____

_____

_____

_____

_____

_____

_____

_____

_____

_____

_____

WHAT PAIN CHANGED JOURNAL:

_____

_____

_____

_____

_____

_____

_____

_____

_____

_____

_____

_____

_____

_____

_____

_____

_____

_____

_____

_____

_____

_____

WHAT PAIN CHANGED JOURNAL:

_____

_____

_____

_____

_____

_____

_____

_____

_____

_____

_____

_____

_____

_____

_____

_____

_____

_____

_____

_____

_____

_____

_____

WHAT PAIN CHANGED JOURNAL:

_____

_____
_____
_____
_____
_____
_____
_____
_____
_____
_____
_____
_____
_____
_____
_____
_____
_____
_____
_____
_____
_____
_____

WHAT PAIN CHANGED JOURNAL:

_____

_____

_____

_____

_____

_____

_____

_____

_____

_____

_____

_____

_____

_____

_____

_____

_____

_____

_____

_____

_____

WHAT PAIN CHANGED JOURNAL:

_____

_____
_____
_____
_____
_____
_____
_____
_____
_____
_____
_____
_____
_____
_____
_____
_____
_____
_____
_____
_____
_____

WHAT PAIN CHANGED JOURNAL:

_____

_____
_____
_____
_____
_____
_____
_____
_____
_____
_____
_____
_____
_____
_____
_____
_____
_____
_____
_____
_____

WHAT PAIN CHANGED JOURNAL:

_____

_____

_____

_____

_____

_____

_____

_____

_____

_____

_____

_____

_____

_____

_____

_____

_____

_____

_____

_____

_____

_____

WHAT PAIN CHANGED JOURNAL:

_____

_____

_____

_____

_____

_____

_____

_____

_____

_____

_____

_____

_____

_____

_____

_____

_____

_____

_____

_____

_____

_____

_____

WHAT PAIN CHANGED JOURNAL:

WHAT PAIN CHANGED JOURNAL:

_____

_____

_____

_____

_____

_____

_____

_____

_____

_____

_____

_____

_____

_____

_____

_____

_____

_____

_____

_____

_____

_____

_____

_____

_____

_____

WHAT PAIN CHANGED JOURNAL:

_____

_____

_____

_____

_____

_____

_____

_____

_____

_____

_____

_____

_____

_____

_____

_____

_____

_____

_____

_____

_____

_____

_____

_____

WHAT PAIN CHANGED JOURNAL:

_____

_____
_____
_____
_____
_____
_____
_____
_____
_____
_____
_____
_____
_____
_____
_____
_____
_____
_____
_____
_____
_____
_____

BOOK VOLUMES: Available on Amazon

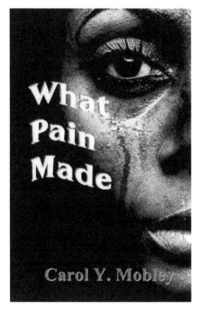

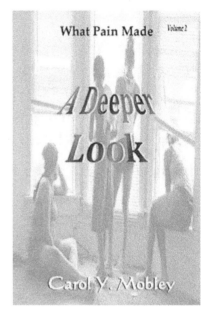

Printed in the USA
CPSIA information can be obtained
at www.ICGtesting.com
CBHW050007310724
12436CB00069B/1478